5 STEPS TO DRAWING
FACES

by Susan Kesselring • illustrated by Dana Regan

The Child's World

Published by The Child's World®
1980 Lookout Drive • Mankato, MN 56003-1705
800-599-READ • www.childsworld.com

ACKNOWLEDGMENTS
The Child's World®: Mary Berendes, Publishing Director
The Design Lab: Design and production
Red Line Editorial: Editorial direction

ISBN: 978-1-60973-197-7
LCCN: 2011927706

Printed in the United States of America
Mankato, MN
July 2011
PA02088

TABLE OF CONTENTS

SKIN AND EYES

Faces come in many different shapes and colors. Our faces are covered with skin. Our skin has **melanin** in it. Melanin gives your skin its color. If you have a lot of melanin, you have darker skin. If you have very little, you have lighter skin. Melanin protects your skin from the sun. People from very warm places tend to have more melanin in their skin. People from cooler places tend to have less.

Eyes come in different shapes and colors, too. The **iris** is the colored part of your eye. This muscle controls how much light enters your eye. The **pupil** is the black spot in the middle of your eye. Light enters your eye through the pupil. When you are in a bright place, the iris squeezes together. Your pupil gets smaller to let in less light. The iris stretches wider when you are in a dark place. Your pupil gets bigger to let in more light.

NOSE

Your nose has two important jobs. One job is breathing. Your nose brings air in and out of your lungs. It warms the air so it doesn't hurt your lungs. Tiny hairs in your nose help stop dirt and dust from getting into your lungs.

The other job is smelling. Your nose has many tiny cells that know different smells. The cells catch smells floating through the air. The cells send a message to your brain. Your brain tells you, "Someone's baking cookies!"

MOUTH

Your mouth has more than one job, too. Your tongue helps you taste food. Your taste buds let your brain know if your food is sweet, salty, sour, or bitter.

Your mouth helps break down the food you eat. Your teeth, tongue, and **saliva** work together. They break your food into tiny pieces that are easy to swallow.

Your lips, tongue, and teeth work together to help you speak. You also use your mouth to give kisses to people you love!

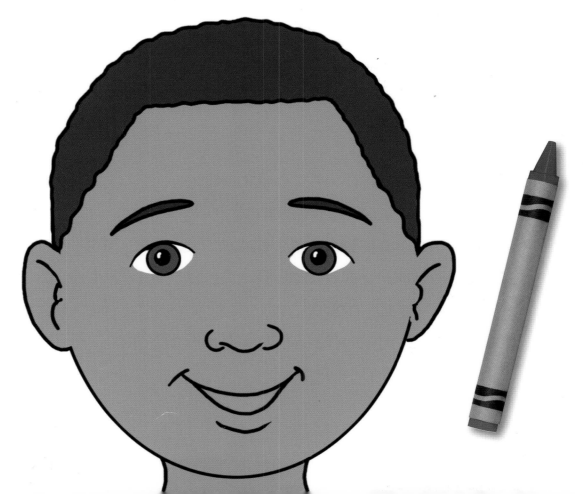

DRAWING TIPS

You've learned about faces. You're almost ready to draw them. But first, here are a few drawing tips:

Every artist needs tools. To learn how to draw faces, you will need:

- Some paper
- A pencil
- An eraser
- Markers, crayons, colored pencils, or watercolors (optional)

Anyone can learn to draw. You might think only some people can draw. That's not true. Everyone can learn to draw. It takes practice, though. The more you draw, the better you will be. With practice, you will become a true artist!

Everyone makes mistakes. This is okay! Mistakes help you learn. They help you know what not to do next time. Mistakes can even make your drawing more special. It's all right if you draw the eyebrows too big. Now you've got a one-of-a-kind drawing. You can erase a mistake you don't like, too. Then start again!

Stay loose. Relax your body before you begin. Hold your pencil lightly. Don't rest your wrist on the table. Instead, move your whole arm as you draw. This will help you make smooth lines. Press lightly on the paper when you draw or erase.

Drawing is fun! The most important thing about drawing is to have fun. Be creative. Your drawings don't have to look exactly like the pictures in this book. Try changing the shape of the eyes. You can also use markers, crayons, colored pencils, or watercolors to bring your faces to life.

1

2

EYES

3

4

Melanin gives your irises their color. Brown is the most common color for eyes. Green is the least common color.

1

2

NOSE

3

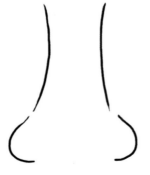

4

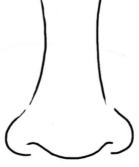

Your nose has two holes called nostrils. Between the nostrils is the septum. This is made of bone and rubbery stuff called **cartilage**. The tip of your nose is made of cartilage, too.

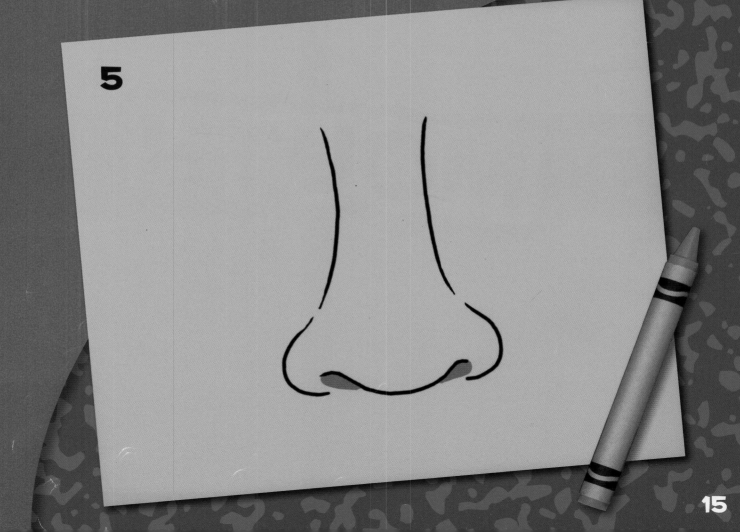

1

2

MOUTH

3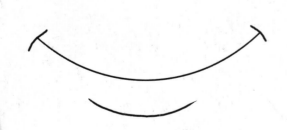

4

Your mouth has many parts. Each part has its own job to do. When you smile, others may see your lips, teeth, and sometimes your gums.

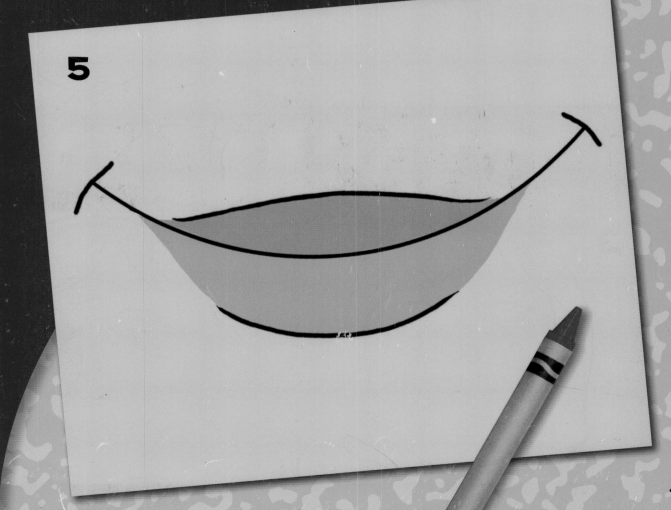

5

1

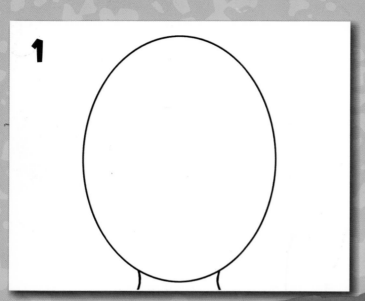

2

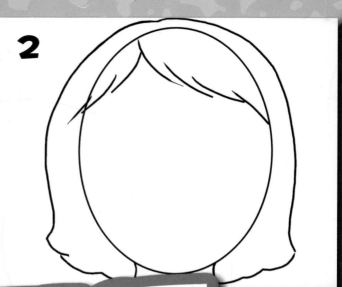

PLAIN FACE

3

4

Eyelashes and eyebrows are part of the way your face looks.
Eyelashes and eyebrows help keep dust and dirt out of your eyes.

1

2

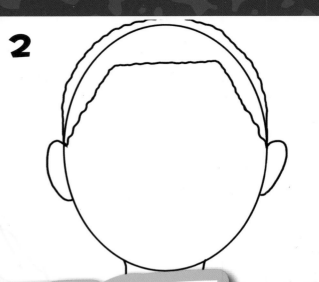

HAPPY FACE

3

4

Make a happy face. Did you feel the corners of your mouth turn up into a smile? Did you notice that your cheeks moved up, too?

5

1

2

SAD FACE

3

4

Make a sad face. Did the corners of your mouth turn down? Did your chin pull up a little bit? Sometimes people's eyebrows turn up when they are sad.

5

1

2

SCARED FACE

3

4

24

Make a scared face. Did you feel your eyes get wider? What did your mouth do? Some people make an *O* with their mouths when they are scared.

5

1

2

SILLY FACE

3

4

Make a silly face. You can do it any way you like. Some people stick out their tongues and cross their eyes.

MORE DRAWING

Now you know how to draw faces. Here are some ways to keep drawing them.

Faces come in all different colors, shapes, and sizes. You can draw them all! Try using pens or colored pencils to draw and color in details. Experiment with crayons and markers to give lips and eyes different colors. You can also paint your drawings. Watercolors are easy to use. If you make a mistake, you can wipe it away with a damp cloth. Try tracing the outline of your drawing with a crayon or a marker. Then paint over it with watercolor. What happens?

Drawing Real Faces

When you want something new to draw, just look around. Faces are everywhere. Ask if you can draw someone's face. He or she can sit still while you work. First, study the face carefully. Is it round or square? Is the nose small or large? What color is the skin? If you need help, use the examples in this book to guide you.

GLOSSARY

cartilage (KAR-tuh-lij): Cartilage is the strong, elastic tissue that connects bones. The tip of the nose is made of cartilage.

iris (EYE-riss): An iris is the round, colored part of the eye. Brown is the most common iris color.

melanin (MEL-uh-nin): Melanin is various colors of pigments found in animals and plants. Melanin gives skin its color.

pupil (PYOO-pul): A pupil is the round, black part of the eye that lets in light. The pupil can become smaller and bigger based on how much light there is.

saliva (suh-LY-vuh): Saliva is the clear liquid in the mouth. Saliva helps break down food.

FIND OUT MORE

BOOKS

Emberley, Ed. *Ed Emberley's Drawing Book: Make a World*. New York: Little Brown, 2006.

Snow, Peggy, and Todd Snow. *Feelings to Share from A to Z*. Oak Park Heights, MN: Maren Green Publishing, 2007.

Soloff Levy, Barbara. *How to Draw Faces*. Mineola, NY: Dover Publications, 2003.

WEB SITES

Visit our Web site for links about drawing faces:

childsworld.com/links

Note to Parents, Teachers, and Librarians: We routinely verify our Web links to make sure they are safe and active sites. So encourage your readers to check them out!

INDEX

ABOUT THE AUTHOR:
Susan Kesselring loves children, books, nature, and her family. She teaches K-1 students in a progressive charter school in Castle Rock, Minnesota.

ABOUT THE ILLUSTRATOR:
Dana Regan earned a bachelor of fine arts from Washington University in St. Louis, Missouri. She is a freelance illustrator and has illustrated more than 70 children's books. She works on her computer using Photoshop to draw and color her digital illustrations.